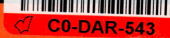

Who Likes Water?

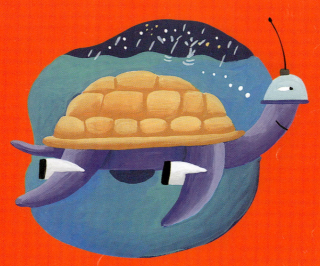

Written by Art Sipowitz
Illustrated by Fraser Williamson

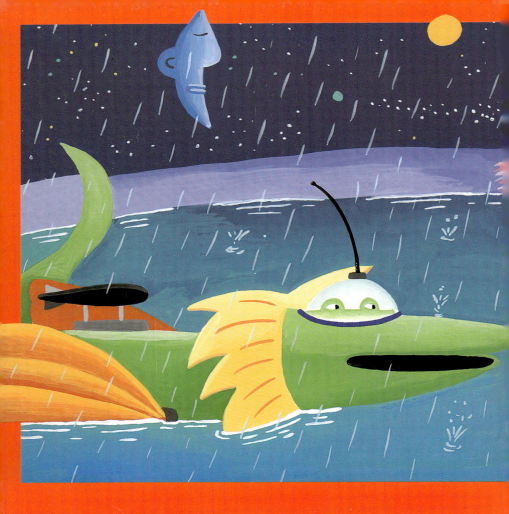

"I do," said the boy.

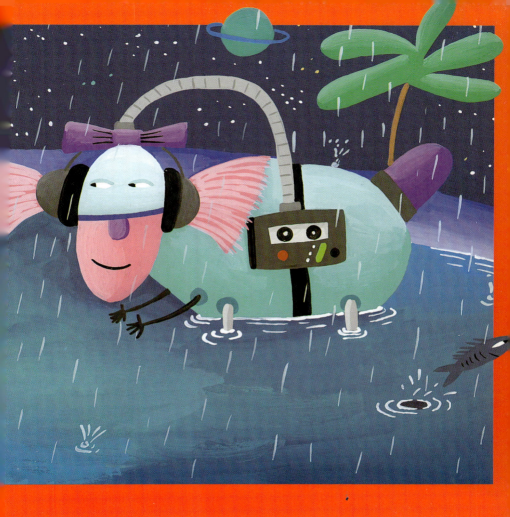

"I do," said the girl.

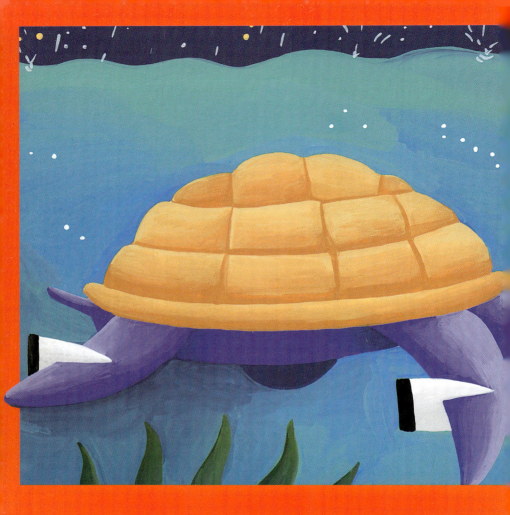

"I do," said the turtle.

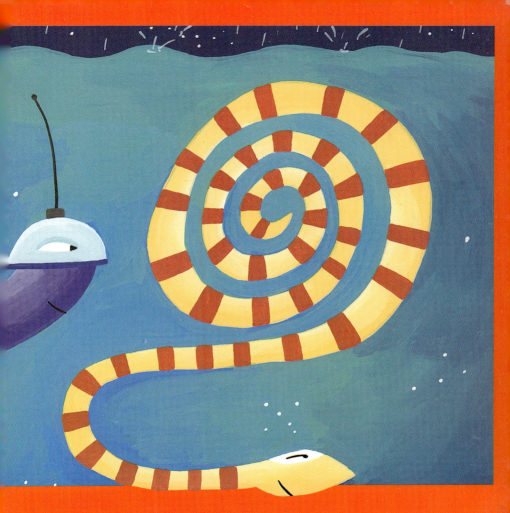

"I do," said the snake.

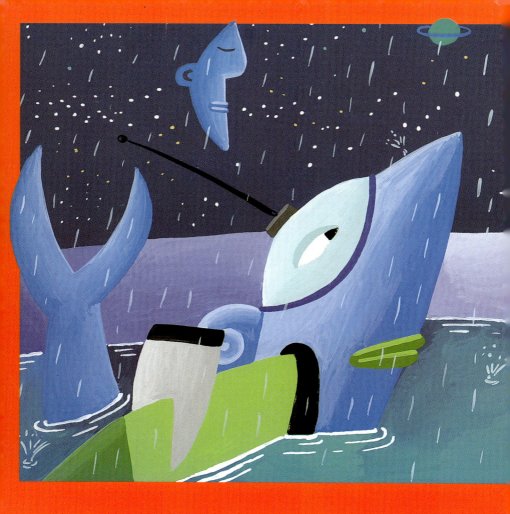

"I do," said the fish.

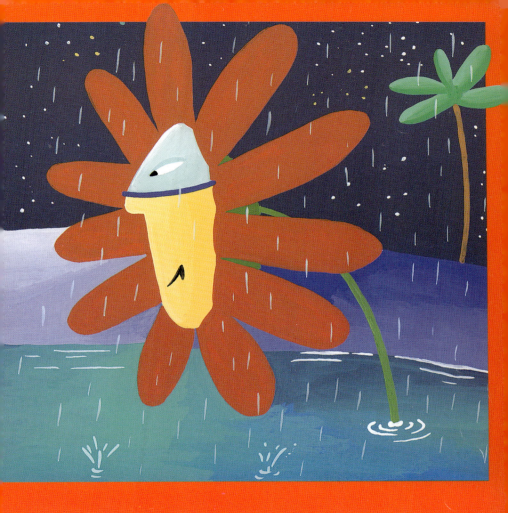

"I do," said the flower.

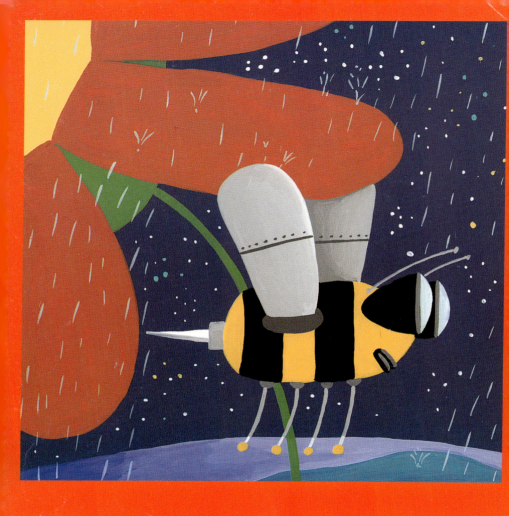

"Not me!" said the bee.